The Jazz Vocalists

A tribute to the singers and the songs of the Jazz and Swing Eras.

Over 80 timeless treasures as sung by Tony Bennett, Ray Charles, Nat 'King' Cole, Bing Crosby, Ella Fitzgerald, Billie Holiday, Lena Horne, the Ink Spots, Peggy Lee, Julie London, Carmen McRae, The Mills Brothers, Anita O'Day, Frank Sinatra, Jo Stafford, Mel Tormé, Sarah Vaughn, Joe Williams, and many more.

Amsco Publications
New York/London/Sydney

Cover photograph by Comstock, Inc.
Compiled and Edited by Ronny S. Schiff
Editorial Design by Elyse Morris Wyman
Interior photography from Starline Productions
the Wayne Knight Collection

This book Copyright © 1997 by Amsco Publications,
A Division of Music Sales Corporation, New York

Order No. AM 92127
US International Standard Book Number: 0.8256.1413.9
UK International Standard Book Number: 0.7119.4340.0

Exclusive Distributors:
Music Sales Corporation
257 Park Avenue South, New York, NY 10010 USA
Music Sales Limited
8/9 Frith Street, London W1V 5TZ England
Music Sales Pty. Limited
120 Rothschild Street, Rosebery, Sydney, NSW 2018, Australia

Printed in the United States of America by
Vicks Lithograph and Printing Corporation

The Singers and The Songs

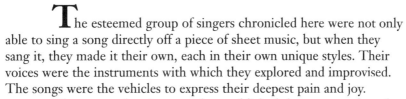

"Jazz is communication—it's a person telling someone else his happiness or sadness or what's happening with him."
—*Billy Eckstine*

The esteemed group of singers chronicled here were not only able to sing a song directly off a piece of sheet music, but when they sang it, they made it their own, each in their own unique styles. Their voices were the instruments with which they explored and improvised. The songs were the vehicles to express their deepest pain and joy.

There were the pioneers who established the new art of vocal jazz in the twenties: blues singers such as Bessie Smith; New Orleans style singers epitomized by Louis Armstrong; the beautiful-voiced Ethel Waters; and the father of scat singing, Cab Calloway. Records, primarily "race records" (recordings by African-American artists), brought the first vocal jazz to the public's attention. In the early thirties, radio increased jazz's impact and gave rise to the talents of Bing Crosby, Ella Fitzgerald, and Billie Holiday. By the end of the war, vocal jazz was a recognized art form; the voice a recognized instrument in jazz. The vocalists stayed in step with the instrumental styles of the times: swing, bebop, cool jazz, and fusion, and sometimes created their own styles, especially in vocal groups.

African-American jazz vocalists didn't have it easy. Many toured under the auspices of the Theatre Owners' Booking Association (TOBA, known as "Tough On Black Asses") who booked the black theatres. Most had to stay in different hotels from their white counterparts in the bands, especially in the South, a situation that occurred as late as the mid sixties in places like Las Vegas. Even as late as the fifties, Nat Cole was attacked on a Birmingham, Alabama, stage for performing with white artists. He once waited all evening in the lobby of a posh New York hotel until 1 AM to get a room. While playing with Earl Hines in Boston in the forties, Billy Eckstine started a brawl when someone in the audience hurled a racial epithet.

Record company executives and producers were absolutely pivotal to the careers of the singers. John Hammond—producer, entrepreneur, and kingpin at Columbia and later president of various labels—produced Bessie Smith's last session and Billie Holiday's first. He was responsible for nurturing the careers of jazz, folk, and pop greats until the mid eighties. Producer and manager Norman Granz established the "Jazz At The Philharmonic" concerts in the forties with a series of memorable recordings to match. His Verve label was the home to many of jazz's finest, including vocalists Billie Holiday, Anita O'Day, and Ella Fitzgerald (whom he also managed).

Another jazz label, Commodore, was founded by Milt Gabler, who also cut some Billie Holiday sides. Later, he broadened Decca's jazz artist roster including vocalists such as Louis Jordan. At Capitol Records, Johnny Mercer—a singer himself—had a fabulous ear for vocalists. RCA had a full slate of race records in the thirties; followed by the establishment of Blue Note in '39, and Savoy in '42. Mercury had its EmArcy jazz division in the fifties, and there were numerous other labels devoted wholly to jazz.

The great jazz historian, Nat Hentoff, stated that, of all forms of music, "jazz is the most self-revealing, the music where there is the least room for the performer to hide who he or she is." Nowhere is this truer than in vocal jazz. These are the people who have bared their souls for us.

Left, top to bottom: *Duke Ellington, Frank Sinatra, Anita O'Day, Billie Holiday.*
Right, top to bottom: *Pearl Bailey, Billy Eckstine and Lena Horne, Cab Calloway, Nat Cole Trio*

Contents

The Birth of Jazz Vocals

The earliest star kudos given to **Cab Calloway** stemmed from his appearance in the 1929 revue *Hot Chocolates* (one of a series of revues featuring African-American performers that ran through the twenties). His headlining Cotton Club engagement, which began in '31, also included a long-running radio program emanating from the Club. In the early thirties, he perfected the art of scat singing, punctuated with his signature "hi-de-ho." So influential was he that he even included a list of hip jazz terms list in his songbook to clue people in to the current jive talk. He had a vast vocal range from a strong bass to a wailing falsetto. With his excellent jazz band, he was a nightclub and motion picture favorite by the mid-thirties and continued performing with unbelievable energy until his death in '94. He recorded: **"Fifteen Minute Intermission"** (1940).

In 1926, **Bing Crosby** and his sidekick Al Rinker drove from Washington to L.A. to see Rinker's sister Mildred Bailey perform; they decided to stay when Bailey was able to get them a singing job. Bandleader Paul Whiteman heard Crosby and Rinker at the Metropolitan Theater in Los Angeles and liked what he heard. Whiteman polished the duo's act for his very sophisticated audiences by teaming them with Harry Barris and dubbing the trio "The Rhythm Boys." The audiences loved Crosby, although he was a handful for Whiteman, and Crosby benefited from working with fine jazzmen like trumpeter Bix Beiderbecke and singer Red McKenzie. In 1927, Crosby cut his first solo recording, "Muddy Water," with Whiteman's group and made it to the charts. He also appeared in the landmark film *The King of Jazz* with Whiteman in 1930 and then struck out on his own. His warm, deep tone and his sense of swing wowed audiences both live and on the radio, and helped launch his long film career.

He recorded: **"Blue Prelude"** (1933), **"But Beautiful"** (1948), **"Imagination," "It's the Talk of the Town," "Like Someone in Love"** (1945), **"My Kinda Love," "Personality"** (1946), **"Shoe Shine Boy," "Sunday, Monday or Always"** (1943), **"Swinging on a Star"** (1944), and **"You Don't Have To Know The Language"** (with The Andrew Sisters—1948).

A popular band singer in the twenties, **Johnny Marvin**'s recordings were light, "up tunes" with a beat. He later wrote songs for Gene Autry movies. He recorded **"Breezin' Along with the Breeze"** (1926).

Russ Columbo was a handsome, popular, romantic singer in the style of Bing Crosby, with hits appearing on the charts from '31 to '34 including **"Prisoner of Love"** in 1932, which he co-wrote and **"All of Me."** He died in an accidental pistol shooting.

Ladies in a Class of Their Own

One of the most revered jazz singers of all time, **Billie Holiday** was discovered in 1933 by jazz recording producer and entrepreneur, John Hammond who noted that she had "an uncanny ear, an excellent memory for lyrics, and she sang with an exquisite sense of phrasing." She recorded one hit with Benny Goodman, and then joined Teddy Wilson's group. She stayed with Wilson from 1935–1938, and afterwards sang with Count Basie and Artie Shaw. She was the one responsible for making jazz singing a recognized art form. She had a voice with an "edge"—she could swing, and yet her voice was both intimate and

---

Photos from the top: *Cab Calloway, Russ Columbo, Bing Crosby*

intense. The musicians loved working with her. She'd trade choruses with them, as if she was playing a horn (though early in her career it was said club owners preferred her to sing songs straight, rather than improvise). "Me, Myself And I" was one of the results of her teaming with saxophonist Lester Young. He was the one who made her royalty, dubbing her "Lady Day." She called him "Prez" (for president), and they made unforgettable recordings together.

The rigors of touring in the racist climate of the late thirties convinced Holiday to remain in New York where she performed frequently at Café Society and made several recordings. She worked with consummate jazz producer and Commodore Record head Milt Gabler in the mid forties—a period when she recorded more and more slow, sad ballads—bringing her a huge following and concerts at New York's large-capacity Town Hall. Her life turned sad as well: arrest and incarceration for a heroin habit took its toll on her health and ability to perform in certain types of clubs (where drug offenders were not permitted to perform). She persevered, making recordings with Stan Getz and signing with Norman Granz's Verve label in '53. Holiday's last great recordings were on Verve where she recorded until her death in July of 1959.

She recorded **"All of Me," "But Beautiful," "Darn That Dream," "Everything Happens To Me," "Imagination," "I Thought about You," "I Wonder Where Our Love Has Gone," "Me, Myself and I"** (1937), **"That Ole Devil Called Love," "Violets for Your Furs,"** and **"We'll Be Together Again."**

Dubbed "The Queen Of Jazz Singers," **Ella Fitzgerald** was introduced to the public when she won the Harlem Amateur Hour in 1934. Shortly afterward, at age seventeen, she was hired by Chick Webb to sing with his Orchestra. Webb became her musical mentor and her legal guardian. She entered the charts in 1936, and a made splash in 1938 with a song she co-wrote, "A-Tisket, A-Tasket," which made her scatting abilities legendary. After Webb died, she took over his band for three years and then went solo. She was one of four other artists who charted in 1940 with **"Imagination."** She recorded **"Into Each Life Some Rain Must Fall"** in 1944 with the Ink Spots—it hit Number 1 and stayed on the charts for over four months.

During this period critics praised her for her impeccable delivery, clear enunciation, and light warm tone, at times even delicate and girlish. Fitzgerald kept honing her improvisational skills, adding to her jazz repertoire the new sound of bebop, but she could always swing. In the fifties she recorded a series of "Songbooks"—each recording dedicated to a singular songwriter or songwriting team. These were particularly successful because of her ability to interpret the vivid lyrics of gifted songwriters. Frequently honored by her the jazz community, she was also the winner of the *down beat* poll for Top Female Vocalist over twenty times.

She also recorded **"All of Me," "Angel Eyes," "Everything Happens to Me," "The Frim Fram Sauce," "Gotta Be This or That," "Here's That Rainy Day," "I Thought about You," "I Wonder Where Our Love Has Gone," "No Moon at All," "Satin Doll," "Show Me the Way To Get Out of This World," "That Ole Devil Called Love," "That's My Desire," "Tuxedo Junction," "Under a Blanket of Blue,"** and **"We'll Be Together Again."**

Photos from the top: *Billie Holiday, Ella Fitzgerald*

Then They Began To Swing

Billy Eckstine sang originally with Earl Hines in late thirties, and then formed his own band, which, through the years, featured musicians such as Charlie Parker, Dizzy Gillespie, Art Blakey, Fats Navarro, and Miles Davis, with Eckstine and Sarah Vaughan as vocalists. His jazz-based style crossed over into bop and then into lush ballads. His phrasing was that of an instrumentalist. He became known for his distinctive deep, rich and seductive, baritone voice with its strong vibrato; a voice so gorgeous that it was described variously as "ripe, sumptuous, and luxuriant." His suave, handsome appearance gave him a romantic image that broke color lines in the forties, making him the first African-American matinee idol.

From the mid forties to the mid fifties, all of his hits made the Top 30 on the charts (**"Prisoner of Love"** made it to Number 10 in 1946; "Lost In Loveliness" in '54 was his last in the Top 30). His 1960 recording of **"Lush Life"** was done in a Las Vegas lounge with a small group. It was included on what some dub as his best recording, *No Cover No Minimum.* Eckstine continued working and recording just before his death in 1993. He also recorded **"All of Me," "Here's That Rainy Day," "There Are Such Things,"** and **"You've Got Me Crying Again."**

Pearl Bailey started on the club circuit in Washington, D.C., in the thirties and moved to New York City, where she established a loyal following in the cabarets and nightclubs. Her initial big break as a singer was with Cootie Williams' band. Her part on Broadway in *St. Louis Woman* led to her career in film, TV and recording. She was a consummate club performer with her rich, expressive, alto and bluesy, relaxed style, offering great patter—often spicy—between the songs. Later in life she established an equally devoted group of fans in Las Vegas. She died in 1990. She recorded **"Diamonds Are a Girl's Best Friend,"** and **"Here's That Rainy Day."**

Lena Horne began her career in clubs, notably the Cotton Club, but, like many singers of the time, got her real boost playing with Noble Sissle's Orchestra in the mid thirties. She appeared with Lew Leslie's *Blackbirds* (one of the many all African-American revues of the twenties and thirties), and made her first album for RCA Victor, entitled *Birth Of The Blues.* She further developed her style with Charlie Barnet's Orchestra, and through radio appearances on NBC's *Dixie* program in 1941. In the early forties, she signed as MGM's token Negro starlet. She refused to play stereotyped African-American roles of the time (maids, pickaninnies), instead managing a few glamour roles that highlighted her unusual singing style and pianistic phrasing. Her ensuing solo albums and the growth and polish of her vocal interpretations, especially her sultry, satiny sound, owe a debt to her gifted musician/arranger husband, Lennie Hayton.

Horne starred in *Jamaica* on Broadway in 1957, and returned to Broadway with her triumphal one-woman, biographical show, *Lena Horne: The Lady And Her Music* in the eighties.

She recorded **"Blue Prelude," "But Beautiful," "Diamonds Are a Girl's Best Friend," "Imagination," "It's Anybody's Spring," "Like Someone in Love," "Polka Dots and Moonbeams," "Prisoner of Love," "Sleigh Ride in July,"** and **"You Don't Have to Know the Language."**

Photos from the top: *Billy Eckstine, Pearl Bailey, Lena Horne, Helen O'Connell*

In The Big Band Spotlight

Helen O'Connell was the featured vocalist with Jimmy Dorsey and his Orchestra from 1939-43, often in duets with Bob Eberly. Their pairing continued into television with Ray Anthony. She recorded **"All of Me," "Imagination,"** and **"Let's Get Away from It All."**

Arranger, orchestrator or composer for several of the songs herein, **Matt Dennis'** first gig was playing with the Horace Heidt Orchestra. By the early forties, he was the arranger/composer with the Tommy Dorsey band, and he played with the Glenn Miller Orchestra during the War. After the War, he opened the Lighthouse Jazz Club in Hermosa Beach, California—a club that became a jazz landmark. He made his first recordings as a vocalist with Paul Weston's orchestra and with Benny Goodman. In 1955, he starred in his own NBC Television network show that featured pop and jazz musicians and singers. He wrote **"Angel Eyes," "Everything Happens to Me," "Let's Get Away from It All," "The Night We Called It a Day," "Violets for Your Furs,"** and **"Will You Still Be Mine?"**

June Christy established herself initially as a big band singer working with society bands in Chicago. Her career blossomed during stint with the Stan Kenton band in 1945, where she followed Anita O'Day as Stan Kenton's band singer. She appeared on all of Kenton's charting hits from 1945 to 1948; "Tampico" was their biggest hit. When Kenton's band changed (as it often did) in the late forties, she went solo, occasionally appearing with Kenton's new bands, and with Bob Cooper and Pete Rugolo. Her clean yet sensual voice, with an even vibrato and a great deal of control, made her a good ballad singer. She recorded **"Angel Eyes," "Aren't You Glad You're You," "Daddy," "Here's That Rainy Day," "The Night We Called It a Day,"** and **"You Say You Care."**

Peggy Lee's big break came with the Benny Goodman Orchestra in early forties. The '41 Goodman group of musicians was spectacularly solid and Lee augmented them well. She'd sung briefly with crooning bandleader Will Osborne before Goodman heard her in a Chicago cocktail lounge. She was a team player, understanding the importance of musical interplay with the musicians. Much was made of her ability to phrase and improvise, her rhythmic acuity, and her sensual voice. She sang everything—including pop, and even comedy numbers—but was best at sultry jazz. Her flair for songwriting become evident throughout years to come when she and her then-husband arranger/band leader Dave Barbour co-wrote several of her songs. She too appeared in films, notably *The Jazz Singer* ('53 version) and *Pete Kelly's Blues*. She recorded **"Satin Doll"** and **"Show Me the Way to Get Out of this World"** (1950).

Frank Sinatra's rise to popularity was swift. He sang in the high school glee clubs in Hoboken, New Jersey, and was inspired to become a professional singer when he saw Bing Crosby perform in a 1936 concert. His group, the Hoboken Four, won the *Major Bowes Original Amateur Radio Hour* in '37, and by '39 he was singing on eighteen different local radio shows in the greater New York area—most often without pay. Tommy Dorsey heard Sinatra when he was singing with Harry James in Chicago and offered him a job, which Sinatra promptly took. Sinatra's wife was due to have a baby, and James, who could not pay as well, was kind enough to let him go. Sinatra wowed the audience the minute he appeared with the Dorsey band. After Sinatra's first week, Dorsey predicted he'd be as big as Crosby. Dorsey, who did his best to provide a comfortable setting for his singers, was a good teacher, helping Sinatra develop his phrasing, breathing, and musical tastes and styles, and Sinatra was eager to learn, improve and broaden his talents.

Within a few months after joining Dorsey, the hits began to flow. Sinatra had his first jaunt onto the *Billboard* charts with **"Polka Dots and Moonbeams,"** from the pens of Johnny Burke and Jimmy Van Heusen, and from the sometimes quirky, sometimes romantic pen of Matt Dennis (**"Everything Happens to me," "Let's Get Away from It All"** in 1941). In 1942, after the record-setting engagement at the Paramount Theatre in New York, where newsreels showed swooning teenagers, Sinatra decided to strike out on his own. He recorded: **"Angel Eyes," "But Beautiful"** (1948), **"Bye Bye Baby," "Close to You"** (1943)," **"A Garden in the Rain," "Gone with the Wind," "Gotta Be This or That," "Here's That Rainy Day," "Imagination"** (1940), **"I Thought about You," "Just as though You Were Here"** (1942), **"Like Someone in Love," "The Night We Called It a Day," "Oh, How I Miss You Tonight," "Polka Dots and Moonbeams"** (1949), **"Prisoner of Love," "Satin Doll," "Snootie Little Cutie," "Somewhere along the Way," "Sunday, Monday or Always"** (1943),**"Swinging on a Star," "There Are Such Things"** (#1, 1943), **"Violets for Your Furs,"** and **"We'll Be Together Again."**

When **Jo Stafford** joined the Pied Pipers in the late thirties, they were an octet. Tommy Dorsey auditioned them for a half-hour radio show, and kept them for two months, but couldn't afford eight singers. Later when the group became a quartet he rehired them. In 1939, Stafford moved on to become the solo ballad singer for Dorsey, singing many of the arrangements by Sy Oliver. Among her unique talents were impeccable pitch and flawless rhythm. She left Dorsey for a solo career, which included over eighty hits on the pop charts from the mid forties to late fifties, most of them with her husband Paul Weston as arranger and bandleader. She recorded **"Diamonds Are a Girl's Best Friend"** (1950), and **"There Are Such Things."**

Although known for his arranging and composition prowess and as a fine big-band trumpeter, **Sy Oliver** often served as a vocalist for several bands including Jimmie Lunceford, Tommy Dorsey, and his own bands well into the 1980s. He recorded **"All of Me," "Bye Bye Baby,"** and **"Yes, Indeed!"** (1941).

Margaret Whiting's career commenced on radio shows in the early forties with Johnny Mercer. As a big-band singer, she could swing flowingly with a clear, impressive voice, and became a featured vocalist with the bands of Freddie Slack, Bill Butterfield and Paul Weston. She had a long string of solo hits in jazz and pop stylings, and charted with both **"In Love in Vain"** (1948) and **"But Beautiful"** (1948/9).

Art Lund, at first known as Art London, started out as the baritone soloist with Benny Goodman. In 1948, he was one of four artists to chart with **"But Beautiful."** (The others were Sinatra, Crosby and Whiting.) Later, he starred in *The Most Happy Fella* on Broadway.

In Their Own Spotlights

Some feel that **Joe Williams**—with his clear, rich, polished baritone—is at his best as a jazz ballad singer, but can he still can *do* the blues! His diction is polished and urbane with sophisticated phrasing. His career started in gospel; his earlier influences then coming from radio, hearing the broadcasts from the Cotton Club and Metropolitan Opera, and he veered into singing with big bands in the late thirties. He sang with Count Basie at the beginning of his career in Chicago,

Page 10, Photos from the top: *June Christy, Peggy Lee, Frank Sinatra*
Page 11, Photos from the top: *Jo Stafford and the Pied Pipers, Sy Oliver, Margaret Whiting, Art Lund.*

along with performing with Fats Waller, Cab Calloway, Fletcher Henderson, Lionel Hampton, and Andy Kirk in the big band years. He was invited to rejoin the Count Basie band in 1954, and he stayed with them until 1961. He continued performing and recording with the greats of jazz—Cannonball Adderley, Coleman Hawkins, Thad Jones and Mel Lewis, George Duke, and so many more, on into the nineties, and even had a recurring stint on *The Cosby Show* in the eighties. He recorded **"Here's That Rainy Day," "It's the Talk of the Town," "Just as though You Were Here,"** and **"You've Got Me Crying Again."**

Remembered now as one of the most prolific lyricists of all times, **Johnny Mercer** was also known as an excellent vocalist, not so much for his voice itself but for his styling. His easygoing, swinging style can be heard especially in his recordings with Paul Weston and the Pied Pipers. Mercer did everything in the music business: sang with Benny Goodman on radio, hosted his own shows with Paul Whiteman as music director, teamed for some vocal duos with Bing Crosby, and wrote with the world's finest songwriters, including jazz greats Billy Strayhorn, Duke Ellington, and Harold Arlen. When he cofounded Capitol Records in 1942, he provided a home for many excellent jazz and pop vocalists, such as Nat "King" Cole, Peggy Lee, and Jo Stafford, as they came off the dwindling big-band circuit. He recorded **"Harmony"** (with Nat "King" Cole—1947), **"Personality"** (1946), and co-wrote **"I Thought about You."**

Nat "King" Cole began his career as a jazz pianist in Chicago, forming the King Cole Trio in 1939. When Cole began singing on his gigs, he felt he didn't have much of a voice or a range, so he interpreted songs like a storyteller with perfect enunciation, warmth, and his signature slight, soft breathy sound. Ray Charles described Cole's baritone voice as "deep and sexy" and noted Cole's repertoire included "jazz improvisation, pretty melodies, hot rhythms and an occasional taste of the blues." Capitol Records' founder Glenn Wallichs signed Cole to his fledgling company in the mid forties. Publishers beat a path to Cole's door to bring him their best tunes. He appeared often in films in the forties and fifties and was the first African-American to host his own TV series. He died far too young in 1965 from lung cancer brought on by a life-long three-pack a day habit.

He recorded **"Angel Eyes," "Baby, Baby All the Time," "Breezin' Along with the Breeze," "But Beautiful," "Everything Happens To me," "The Frim Fram Sauce"** (1946), **"Harmony"** (with Johnny Mercer—1947), **"If Love Is Good to Me"** (1953), **"My Kinda Love," "(There Is) No Greater Love," "No Moon at All" "Oh, How I Miss You Tonight" "Polka Dots and Moonbeams" "Somewhere along the Way"** (1952), **"Sunday, Monday or Always," "There Are Such Things," "There! I've Said It Again,"** and **"Time Out for Tears."**

While working with Pearl Bailey, **Tony Bennett** was given some tips to stardom by Bob Hope. Bennett started his career as a pop singer with a long run of chart singles; his biggest hit was his 1962 pop ballad, "I Left My Heart in San Francisco." He then turned toward jazz, recording with jazz greats Count Basie, Bill Evans, Marion McPartland and Duke Ellington. Thereafter, recording took a back seat to club dates until the mid nineties when he teamed with k.d. lang, appearing on MTV and winning a Grammy in 1995. The *All Music Guide To Jazz* notes that Bennett claims he modeled his phrasing on Art Tatum's piano technique and his warm delivery on Mildred Bailey's vocal style. He recorded **"Angel Eyes," "But Beautiful," "Here's That Rainy Day," "I Thought about You,"** and **"We'll Be Together Again."**

Mel Tormé came along in the mid forties with his vocal group, the Mel-Tones, who performed his amazing arrangements with Artie Shaw's band. With his resonant tenor voice, he became known as the "Velvet Fog." His ability as a great jazz vocal "interpretationist" was complemented by his impeccable musical craftsmanship. He worked and recorded often with pianist George Shearing, as well as with many decades worth of jazz greats. In addition, he acted in films and television, wrote books, and, of course, is known for composing talents, especially for "The Christmas Song." He recorded **"Aren't You Glad You're You," "But Beautiful," "Here's That Rainy Day," "The Night We Called It a Day," "No Moon at All," "Satin Doll,"** and **"Yes, Indeed!"**

Carmen McRae launched her jazz career as a club pianist, therein developing extraordinary timing and pacing. She joined Benny Carter's orchestra in 1944, and sang with Mercer Ellington's and Count Basie's bands in the late forties. Her first recordings, released in the early fifties, earned her *down beat*'s Best New Female Singer award, and she became known for her phrasing, sound rhythmical abilities, vocal inflections, and delivery. Ranking among the top jazz singers, she could and did sing in any genre from pop to standards, from show tunes to scat, and ballads to bebop. She recorded **"Dear Ruby (Ruby My Dear)," "The Frim Fram Sauce," "If Love Is Good to Me," "Imagination," "It Shouldn't Happen to a Dream," "The Night We Called It a Day," "Satin Doll,"** and **"Suddenly (In Walked Bud)."**

Sarah Vaughan's earliest musical experiences, like so many other singers, were in the church choir and in piano lessons with a fortunate plus—the Newark School of the Arts. Jazz was in her blood, and by the early forties she was able to perform on the stage of the Apollo and find immediate mentors in the form of Ella Fitzgerald and Billy Eckstine. Eckstine recommended her for the co-vocalist position with him with Earl Hines' band. She was an instant success, especially with her fellow musicians, who hailed her ability to improvise and harmonize (she said she was more influenced by horns than voices), as well as her precise intonation and rhythmic sense. By 1946 she was performing as a soloist and making recordings that featured some of the world's best jazz musicians. Dubbed "The Divine One" in the fifties, she was performing to worldwide acclaim of her rich, colorful vocal range, her scat singing, and the beauty of her voice.

She recorded **"All of Me," "Broken Hearted Melody"** (1959), **"Close to You," "Darn That Dream," "Don't Go to Strangers," "A Garden in the Rain," "Here's That Rainy Day," "If Love Is Good to Me," "Imagination," "Like Someone in Love," "My Kinda Love," "Polka Dots and Moonbeams," "There Are Such Things,"** and **"You Say You Care."**

Hot Jazz, Cool Jazz

A refined torchy singer in the "cool" genre of fifties jazz, **Chris Connor**'s career was launched in Claude Thornhill's vocal quintet. Thereafter, she joined Stan Kenton's Orchestra on June Christy's recommendation. Her style was described as cool and inviting, and often as soft, silky, and sultry. She was known for altering the rhythms on ballads. From the fifties through the eighties, many of her solo albums—some with Kenton and Maynard Ferguson—and especially her interpretations

Page 12, Photos from the top: *Johnny Mercer, Nat "King" Cole, Tony Bennett, Mel Tormé*
Page 13, Photos from the top: *Carmen McRae, Sarah Vaughan, Al Hibbler, Anita O'Day*

of standards, were very successful. She recorded **"Here's That Rainy Day," "In Love in Vain," "The Night We Called It a Day," "Time Out for Tears,"** and **"We'll Be Together Again."**

Blind from birth, **Al Hibbler** debuted with jazz pianist Jay McShann and then became vocalist with Duke Ellington from 1943 to 1951. In the early fifties, he could be heard in the intense jazz scene that existed in L.A.'s South-Central. Deep-voiced with a vocal resonance that one could almost feel, he crossed over into R&B and then burst onto pop charts with "Unchained Melody." Nevertheless he remained a blues and jazz singer to the end. He recorded **"It's the Talk of the Town," "There Are Such Things,"** and **"(There Is) No Greater Love."**

Morgana King trained as an opera singer, and turned to jazz in the late forties, starting in clubs with small groups and becoming a major supper-club draw by the sixties. She also acted in several films, most notably *The Godfather*. Her opera training has given her the ability to scat uniquely at the top of her very broad range. She recorded **"Imagination," "Like Someone in Love,"** and **"Will You Still Be Mine?"**

With one of the most seductive, sultriest voices of the fifties, beauteous actress **Julie London** was married to *Dragnet's* Jack Webb when she slinked through her only pop hit, "Cry Me A River." However, her next husband, songwriter Bobby Troup encouraged her singing career and a spate of sensual albums with hip arrangements ensued. In the seventies, London was seen with Troup in a non-singing star role on television's *Emergency*. She recorded **"Baby, Baby All the Time," "Daddy," "Diamonds Are a Girl's Best Friend," "Everything Happens to Me,"** and **"There! I've Said It Again."**

Songwriter/entertainer **Bobby Troup** recorded many of his songs, but was himself instrumental in getting them to other jazz artists: While attending the University of Pennsylvania, he wrote and performed **"Daddy"** for their famous *Mask & Wig Show*. By luck he was able to get it to big-band leader Sammy Kaye, who recorded it in '41 and took it to Number 1 on the charts. Shortly afterward, while in the Marine Corps, Troup put on an armed forces show and performed **"Snootie Little Cutie."** He used his track record on "Daddy" as his entrée to get "Snootie Little Cutie" to Tommy Dorsey, who recorded it with his big band. Troup was quick to recognize the young Nat Cole's talents, and he convinced Cole and his trio to record **"Baby, Baby All the Time"** and another one of his tunes, "Route 66."

Anita O'Day's first singing gigs were in Chicago clubs; her big break came when she replaced Irene Daye in Gene Krupa's band in '41. She moved on to the Stan Kenton band in '44. Blessed with an innate sense of rhythm, critics raved about her interpretation, her inventiveness and improvisational ability. Hers is an instrumental voice; that is, she plays it like one of the instruments in the band, often phrasing like a jazz drummer. She was probably the first white woman to scat, but she could sing anything as evidenced by everything from her rendition of "Let Me Off Uptown" with saxophonist Roy Eldridge to her charting version of the country-pop standard "Tennessee Waltz." She too signed with Granz's Verve label and continued her recording career throughout the fifties and into the sixties. Drugs and drinking waylaid her for part of the sixties, but she fought back and recovered to start her own label, Emily, and then to continue to record and perform into the nineties. In 1985, she celebrated her fiftieth anniversary as a jazz artist with a concert at Carnegie Hall.

She recorded **"Angel Eyes," "Blue Champagne," "Here's That Rainy Day," "Like Someone in Love," "The Night We Called It a Day," "No Moon at All," "Opus One,"** and **"Under a Blanket of Blue."**

With his deep and rich baritone voice, **Arthur Prysock** gained fame in the forties and into the fifties with Buddy Johnson's band. He covered R&B, blues, and jazz with equal skill and fervor. His voice was especially impressive in his ballad interpretations. **"Don't Go to Strangers"** appears on his 1965 recording with Count Basie. He also recorded **"I Wonder Where Our Love Has Gone,"** and **"You Always Hurt the One You Love."**

Dakota Staton, developed her style from gospel and jazz instrumentalists, as did Sarah Vaughan and Dinah Washington. Born in Pittsburgh, she sang professionally with her sisters before going solo with her husky and strong voice. Her record deal with Capitol in 1955 brought her smooth delivery, exuberant manner and exceptional scat-singing to the public's attention and earned her *down beat*'s Most Promising Newcomer award. Her albums showed that she could interpret anything from the blues to standards to jazz, and always swing. She recorded **"Everything Happens to Me," "No Moon at All,"** and **"There Are Such Things."**

Primarily a cabaret singer, **Sylvia Syms** was most popular in the sixties, with specialties in ballads and blues, highly stylized standards, and jazz tunes. She recorded **"Here's That Rainy Day."**

Nancy Wilson appeared on the scene in 1959 with the Billy May Orchestra and thereafter turned out an enormous body of work with her signature crisp, lucid, and intricate jazz phrasing in blues, ballad, and jazz genres. Cited as an influence on many pop singers including Anita Baker and Regina Belle, she's continued to release albums into the nineties. She recorded **"Angel Eyes," "Blue Prelude," "But Beautiful," "Darn That Dream," "If Love Is Good to Me," "I Thought about You,"** and **"Satin Doll."**

Jazz with an R&B Flavor

Ray Charles' singing career has encompassed a great many vocal stylings —R&B, country, soul, blues, and jazz. Blind by age seven, he was able to pick out boogie woogie patterns on his neighbor's piano and, with the training at school, he was a master of the keyboard when he reached his teens. After leaving school, he was able to find club jobs throughout the country, eventually settling in Los Angeles. By 1948, he was recording in the style of Nat Cole. His synthesis of gospel, blues and jazz came into its own on his mid fifties Atlantic recordings. **"Yes, Indeed!"** was a perfect choice to illustrate his unique gospel shout, but then he could also caress a ballad like **"Angel Eyes"** (in duo with Willie Nelson). In the nineties he's became known for his Pepsi commercials ("uh-huh!"). His contributions to music were recognized in 1986 at the Kennedy Center Awards presented by President Reagan. He also recorded **"This Love of Mine,"** and **"You've Got Me Crying Again."**

Savannah Churchill sang and recorded both jazz and R&B in the late forties, working with Jimmy Lytell and Benny Carter. **"Time Out for Tears"** charted in 1948. Churchill died in 1974.

Dinah Washington renown was as a superb stylist. Her earliest stylistic influences came from gospel—singing and playing piano in a Chicago church, where she eventually became the choral director. She began singing in local nightclubs in 1942, joining Lionel Hampton's band in 1943. Her rich bluesy phrasing, high clear voice, and gospel-like

---

Page 14, Photos from the top: *Bobby Troup, Julie London, Arthur Prysock, Sylvia Syms*
Page 15, Photos from the top: *Ray Charles, Dinah Washington, The Mills Brothers*

presentation enabled her to cross back and forth between jazz and R&B, as well as landing on the pop charts. With her characteristic "tear" in her voice that would be copied by several R&B singers, her strongest period as a soul singer was in early fifties; then she switched back to jazz styling. She died in 1963 at the age of 39. She recorded **"Accent on Youth," "All of Me," "Don't Go to Strangers," "I Thought about You," "That's My Desire," "Time Out for Tears,"** and **"You've Got Me Crying Again."**

In Harmony—The Groups

The **Mills Brothers**, featuring brothers Herbert, Harry and Donald, entered radio in the late twenties with a smooth, relaxed style (although their first hit was the rousing "Tiger Rag") and charted through to the sixties. Their gentle ballad **"You Always Hurt the One You Love"** was a Number 1 hit for them in 1944, staying on the charts for thirty-three weeks. They were able to imitate instruments vocally; perhaps that's why they were rarely accompanied by anything other than guitar by their brother John (and after his death, by their father John, Sr.). Favorites in clubs, they had hits with Bing Crosby, Ella Fitzgerald, Louis Armstrong, and Sy Oliver's Orchestra. They also recorded **"Imagination," "Oh, How I Miss You Tonight," "Opus One,"** and **"Shoe Shine Boy."**

Enjoying most of their popularity in the forties, the **Ink Spots** consisted of Bill Kenny, Orville Jones (replaced by Herb Kenny), Charlie Fuqua, and Ivory "Deek" Watson (replaced by Billy Bowen). In forties terms their sound was "sweet and hot," and they could swing a ballad with unique harmonies. They also indulged in Cab Calloway-like "hi-de-ho's." Most importantly, they paved the way for many black vocal groups to come. They had a long string of hits, many Number 1, including **"Into Each Life Some Rain Must Fall"** with Ella Fitzgerald in 1944. They recorded **"Prisoner of Love"** (1946) and **"You Can't See the Sun when You're Crying"** (1947).

In the fifties, it was **Hi-Los** who advanced the sound of four-part harmony with singers Clark Burroughs, Bob Morse, Gene Puerling, and Don Shelton. Their sound now could be described as "middle of the road jazz," but they took harmonies to a new place then. (Gene Puerling and Don Shelton also formed Singers Unlimited in the eighties.) They recorded **"But Beautiful," "I Thought about You," "My Sugar Is So Refined," "The Night We Called It a Day,"** and **"There Are Such Things."**

The members of **Manhattan Transfer** were the vocal jazz *wunderkinder* of the seventies. The stylings of Tim Hauser, Alan Paul, Janis Siegel and Cheryl Bentyne (Laurel Masse '72 to '79) established a fine line between pop and jazz. Because of this they enjoyed wide audience appeal with smashing, exuberant concerts and fabulous harmonies. They also influenced the direction of school jazz choirs, infusing new life into the "being" of group harmonies. They recorded **"Blue Champagne," "Fifteen Minute Intermission," "Snootie Little Cutie,"** and **"Tuxedo Junction."**

For more background on many of these great artists see *The Library of Big Band Hits Songbook*, Music Sales Corporation.

Photos from the top: *The Ink Spots, The Hi-Los, Manhattan Transfer*

16

ACCENT ON YOUTH

Words by Tot Seymour, Music by Vee Lawnhurst

love.   Deep down in our hearts   we have learned the   truth,   There's
know.   Love will keep us young   and I proph - e - sy

Moderately slow, a tempo

noth - ing half so pre-cious, dear, as   youth. _____
That old Fa - ther Time will pass us   by. _____

poco rit.

Why   is   the rose   be - gin - ning to bud in spring? __

Why are the birds   be - gin - ning to fly and sing? __   And

18

19

What brings us here con-fess-ing that love is born? Al-

though we call it in-spi-ra-tion, It's just the ac-cent of

youth.

2. I do not youth.

rall.

ALL OF ME

by Seymour Simons and Gerald Marks

one-sid-ed love ___ af-fair? All you took, I

glad-ly gave. There's noth-ing left for me to save.

Chorus:

All of me, ___ Why not take all of me, ___

Can't you see ___ I'm no good with-

23

out you. Take my lips, I want to lose them, Take my arms, I'll nev-er use them. Your good-bye left me with eyes that cry,

24

How can I _____ go on, dear, with -
out you. _____ You took the part that
once was my heart, So why not take all of
me.

me.

ANGEL EYES

by Matt Dennis and Earl Brent

Try to think__ that love's not a-round,__ Still it's un-com-fort-'bly near__

__ My old heart_ ain't gain-in' no ground_ be-cause my an-gel eyes ain't here.__

An-gel eyes_ that old dev-il sent_ they glow un-bear-a-bly bright_

Need I say_ that my love's mis-spent,_ mis-spent with an-gel eyes to-night._

So drink up,_____ all you peo - ple,_ Or-der an-y-thing you see,_

Have fun,_____ you hap-py peo-ple, The drink and the laugh's_ on me._

AREN'T YOU GLAD YOU'RE YOU

Words by Johnny Burke, Music by Jimmy Van Heusen

BABY, BABY ALL THE TIME

by Bobby Troup

BLUE CHAMPAGNE

by Grady Watts, Jimmy Eaton and Frank Ryerson

BLUE PRELUDE

by Joe Bishop and Gordon Jenkins

BREEZIN' ALONG WITH THE BREEZE

by Haven Gillespie, Seymour Simons and Richard A. Whiting

o - ver,   kind - a grew up   wild,   My home's wher - a
burn - in'   ev - 'ry night for   me,   I'm like a

ev - er, I may   be.
bird that's fly - in'   free.

Chorus:

I'm   just breez - in' a - long with the   breeze,

Trail - in' the   rails   roam - in' the   seas.

weary Mother Nature makes me a bed.

I'm just go-in' a-long as I please,

Breez-in' a - long with the

breeze.

breeze.

ritard. e dim.

BROKEN HEARTED MELODY

Music by Sherman Edwards, Lyrics by Hal David

song of love. _____ Now _____ you just keep

taunt - ing me _____ With _____

_____ the mem-o-ry of {his - a / her - a} ten - der love. Oh!

No chord

45

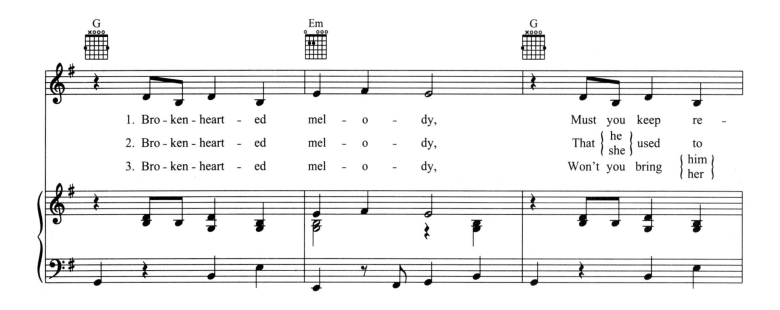

1. Bro - ken - heart - ed mel - o - dy, Must you keep re -
2. Bro - ken - heart - ed mel - o - dy, That {he/she} used to
3. Bro - ken - heart - ed mel - o - dy, Won't you bring {him/her}

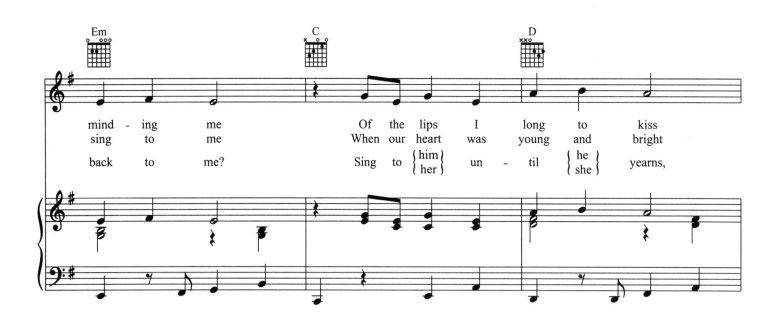

mind - ing me Of the lips I long to kiss
sing to me When our heart was young and bright
back to me? Sing to {him/her} un - til {he/she} yearns,

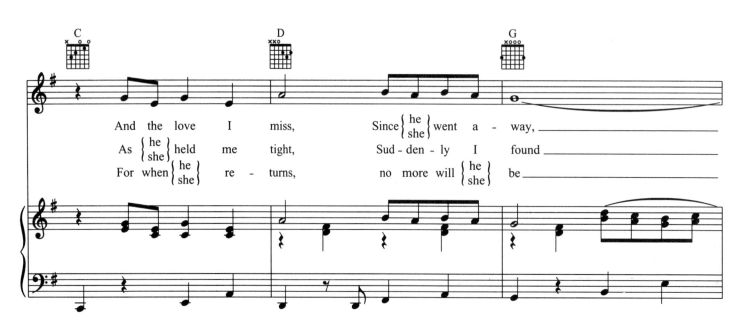

And the love I miss, Since {he/she} went a - way, _____
As {he/she} held me tight, Sud - den - ly I found _____
For when {he/she} re - turns, no more will {he/she} be _____

BUT BEAUTIFUL

by Johnny Burke and Jimmy Van Heusen

CLOSE TO YOU

by Al Hoffman, Jerry Livingston and Carl Lampl

Slowly with a light rhythm

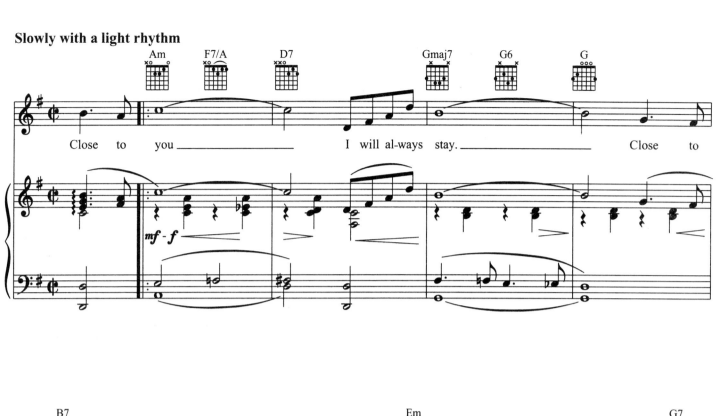

Close to you _____ I will al-ways stay. _____ Close to

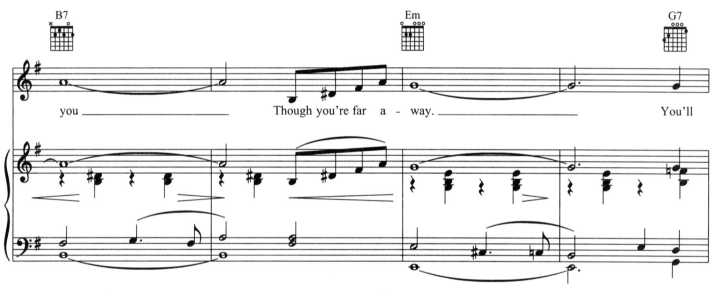

you _____ Though you're far a - way. _____ You'll

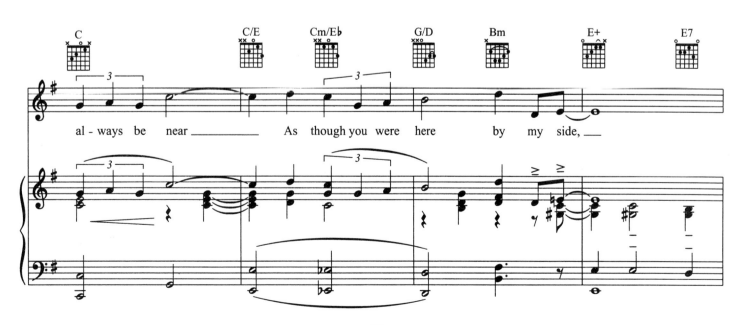

al - ways be near _____ As though you were here by my side, ___

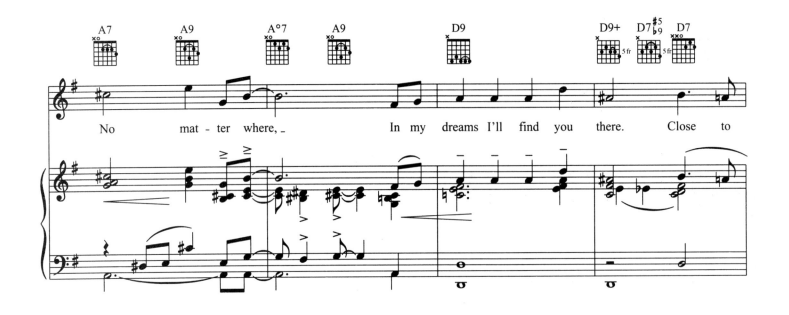

No mat-ter where, _ In my dreams I'll find you there. Close to

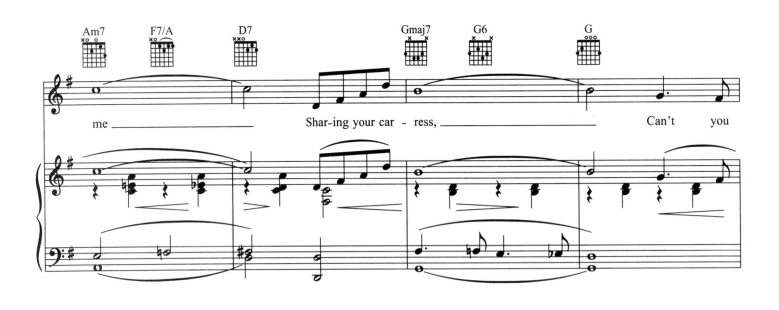

me _____ Shar-ing your car - ress, _____ Can't you

see _____ You're my hap-pi - ness. _____ Where -

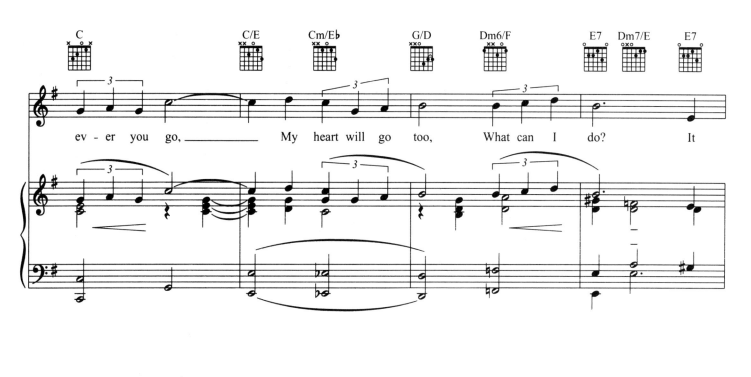

ev - er you go, _____ My heart will go too, What can I do? It

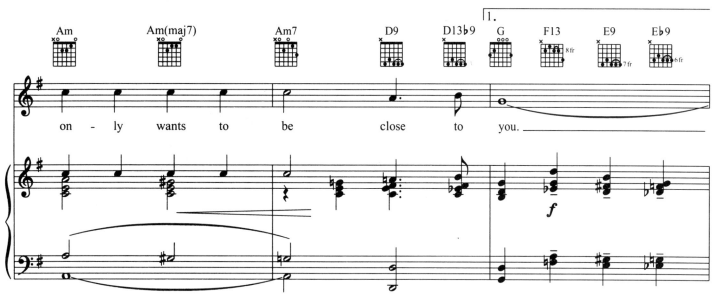

on - ly wants to be close to you. _____

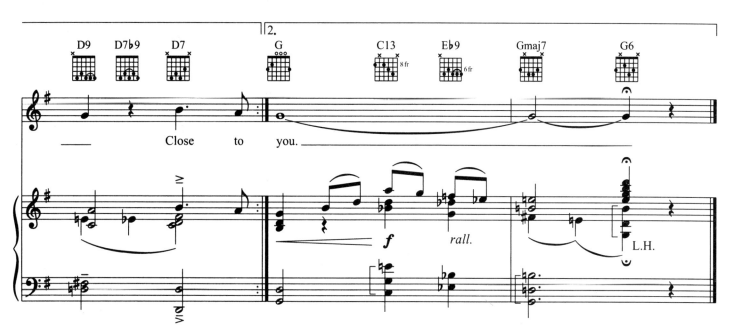

Close to you. _____

BYE BYE BABY
from GENTLEMEN PREFER BLONDES
Words by Leo Robin, Music by Jule Styne

COME SUNDAY
from BLACK, BROWN AND BEIGE

by Duke Ellington

Lord, Dear Lord a - bove: God Al - might - y, God of Love,

Please look down and see my peo - ple through. _____

1. I be - lieve that God put sun and moon up in the
2. Heav - en is a good - ness time, a bright - er light on

* *Alternate rhythm:*

60

DADDY

by Bobby Troup

DON'T GO TO STRANGERS

Words by Redd Evans, Music by Arthur Kent and Dave Mann

DARN THAT DREAM

by Jimmy Van Heusen and Edgar De Lange

DEAR RUBY
(Vocal Version of RUBY, MY DEAR)

Music by Thelonious Monk, Words by Sally Swisher

DIAMONDS ARE A GIRL'S BEST FRIEND
from GENTLEMEN PREFER BLONDES

Words by Leo Robin, Music by Jule Styne

square - cut or pear - shape, these rocks don't lose their shape.
stiff back or stiff knees, you scan straight at Tif - f'ny's.
then that those lous - es go back to their spous - es.

poco a poco cresc.

1. 2.

Dia - monds are a girl's best friend!
Dia - monds are a girl's best friend!

f

f pronounced

Optional additional lyrics:

Verse
    A well-conducted rendezvous
    Makes a maiden's heart beat quicker.
    But when the rendezvous is through,
    These stones still keep their flicker.

Chorus
    Romance is divine, and I'm not one to knock it,
    But diamonds are a girl's best friend!
    Romance is divine, yes, but where can you hock it?
    When the fame is gone,
    Just try and pawn a tired Don Juan!

    Some men buy, and some just sigh
    That to make you their bride they intend.
    But buyers or sighers,
    They're such god-damn liars!
    Diamonds are a girl's best friend!

EVERYTHING HAPPENS TO ME

by Tom Adair and Matt Dennis

Ddim Ebm6 Dm7 G7 Cm7 B7
guess I'm just a fool who nev-er looks be-fore he jumps, EV-RY-THING HAP-PENS TO ME
Bb6 Fm7 Bb+ Ebmaj9 Eb6
At first my heart thot you could break this jinx for me, that
Fm7 Bb7 Ebmaj9 Eb6 Em7 A7+
love would turn the trick to end des-pair, But now I just can't fool this head that
Dmaj9 D6 Gm D+ Gm7 C7 Cm7 F7
thinks for me, I've mort-gaged all my cas-tles in the air I've

tel - e - graphed and phoned, I sent an "Air - mail Spec - ial" too, Your
ans - wer was "Good - by," And there was ev - en pos - tage due, I
fell in love just once and then it had to be with you ___
EV - 'RY - THING HAP - PENS TO ME ___ I

FIFTEEN MINUTE INTERMISSION

by Sunny Skylar and Bette Cannon

With a swinging beat

THE FRIM FRAM SAUCE

Music by Joe Ricardel, Words by Redd Evans

A GARDEN IN THE RAIN

Words by James Dyrenforth, Music by Carroll Gibbons

Lyrics: I re-call a sum-mer's day, when you and I had

strolled a - way, And sud - den - ly a storm drew

nigh. _____ Seek - ing shel - ter

from the rain, we hur - ried down a lit - tle lane, And

found a love - ly sight near - by. _____

poco a poco ritard.

GONE WITH THE WIND

Music by Allie Wrubel, Words by Herb Magidson

Flowingly

Moderately slow (a tempo)

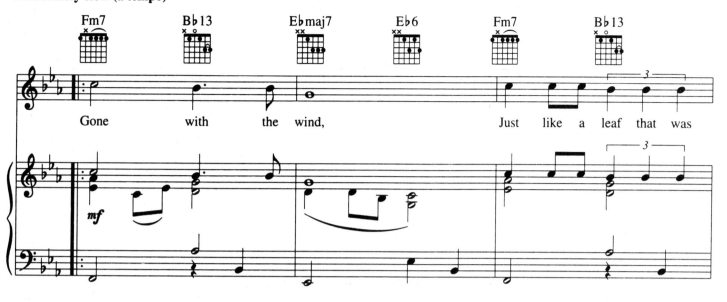

Gone with the wind, Just like a leaf that was

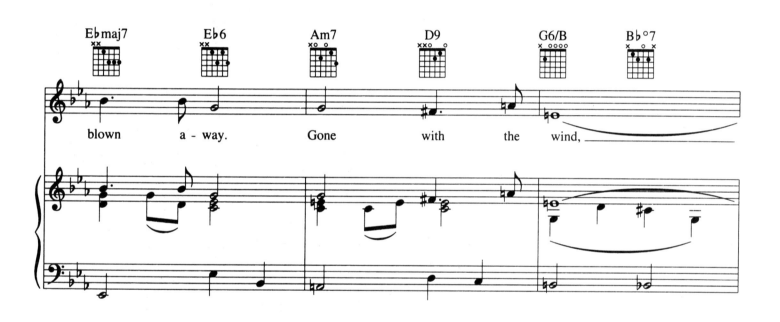

blown a - way. Gone with the wind, ____

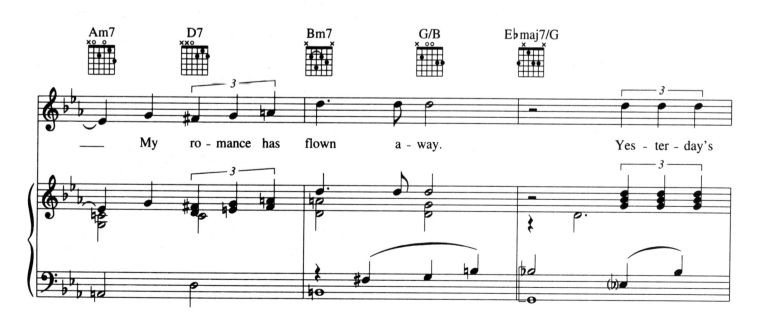

____ My ro - mance has flown a - way. Yes - ter - day's

wind. _____ The glad-ness that filled my heart.

Just like a flame. Love burned bright-ly, then be-

came an emp-ty smoke dream that has gone, gone with the

wind. _____

ritard

105

HARMONY

Words by Johnny Burke, Music by Jimmy Van Heusen

Moderately bright

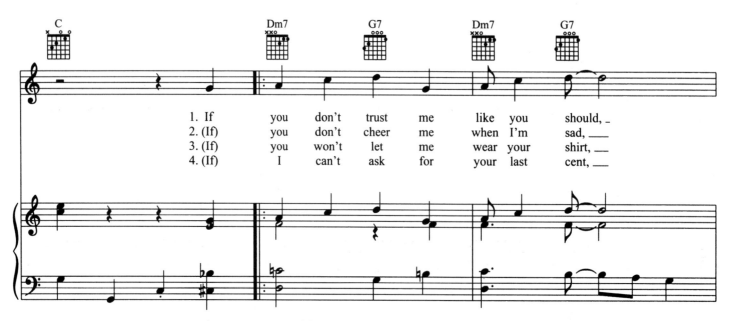

1. If you don't trust me like you should, _
2. (If) you don't cheer me when I'm sad, _
3. (If) you won't let me wear your shirt, _
4. (If) I can't ask for your last cent, _

Min - ne - a - po - lis with - out St. Paul! __ It's har - mo - ny, ___
let - to sound the same with no quar - tet? __ It's har - mo - ny, ___
sar - dines get a - long with such fin - esse? __ It's har - mo - ny, ___
Brig - ham Young get by with no di - vorce? _ It's har - mo - ny, ___

That's all! 2. If
You bet! 3. If
Oh, yes! 4. If

Of course! It's har - mo - ny! ____

GOTTA BE THIS OR THAT

by Sunny Skylar

HERE'S THAT RAINY DAY

by Johnny Burke and Jimmy Van Heusen

I THOUGHT ABOUT YOU

by Johnny Mercer and Jimmy Van Heusen

under the stars, __ A wind-ing stream, _____

Moon shin-ing down __ on some lit-tle town, __ And with each beam __

same old dream. At ev-'ry stop that we made,___ oh, I

thought a-bout you, _____ But when I pulled down the shade,_

120

I WONDER WHERE OUR LOVE HAS GONE

by Buddy Johnson

willing to pay, _____ But, darling, if that's not enough, I'll do anything you say.

Darling, please, _____ wherever you may be, Hear my plea _____ and hurry

back to me. _____ I know without your love I just can't go on, I

wonder where our love has gone. _____

IF LOVE IS GOOD TO ME

Music by Fred Spielman, Words by Redd Evans

Clouds will cry and rain will fall, The earth will sigh and drink it all, If love is good to me. There al-ways will be skies of blue a-bove me, Just as long as Moth-er Na-ture makes you love me.

Leaves will fall from win-ter's chill, And I'll re-call the sum-mer thrill that

once you gave to me. These won - d'rous things each year de-

pend on you, my dear, This all could be if love is good to

1.

me.

2.

me, If love is good to me.

poco rit.

ritard.

IMAGINATION

Words by Johnny Burke, Music by Jimmy Van Heusen

The things my mind makes up ____

CHORUS (*Slowly with a lilt*)
a tempo

IM-AG-I - NA-TION is fun-ny, It makes a cloud-y day sun-ny,

Makes a bee think of hon-ey, Just as I ____ think of you ____ IM-AG-I -

NA-TION is cra-zy, Your whole per-spec-tive gets haz-y,

129

NA - TION is sil - ly, You go a - round wil - ly -

nil - ly. For ex - am - ple, I go a - round want - ing

you_____ And yet, I can't im - ag - ine that you want me

too._____ IM - AG - I - too._____

(Guitar Tacit)

8va bassa

131

IN LOVE IN VAIN

Words by Leo Robin, Music by Jerome Kern

Moderately slow, with expression

133

INTO EACH LIFE SOME RAIN MUST FALL

by Allan Roberts and Doris Fisher

Moderately slow, with a gentle beat

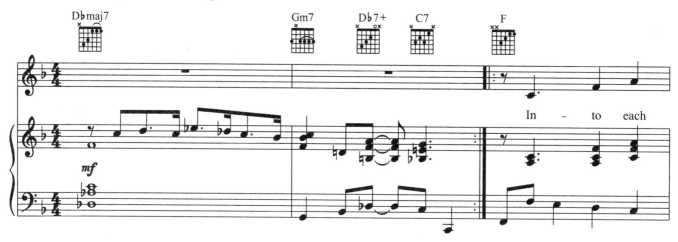

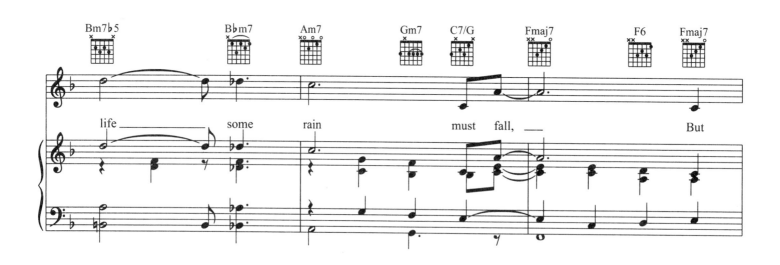

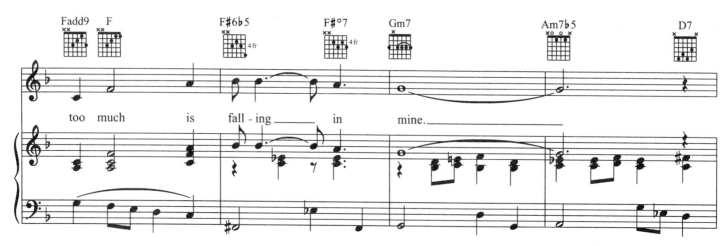

IT SHOULDN'T HAPPEN TO A DREAM

Music by Duke Ellington and Johnny Hodges, Words by Don George

IT'S ANYBODY'S SPRING

by Johnny Burke and Jimmy Van Heusen

IT'S THE TALK OF THE TOWN

by Al Neiburg, Jerry Livingston and Marty Symes

Moderately slow

It's the talk of the town. town.

Instrumental solo

We

151

JUST AS THOUGH YOU WERE HERE

by Edgar DeLange and John Benson Brooks

Freely, with motion

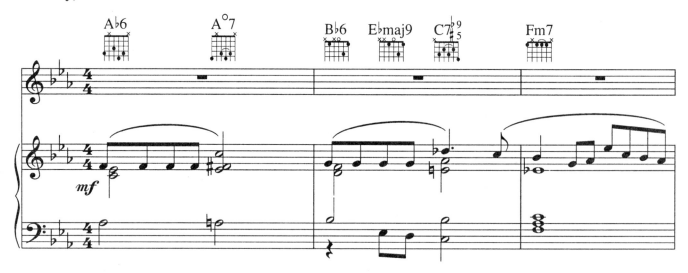

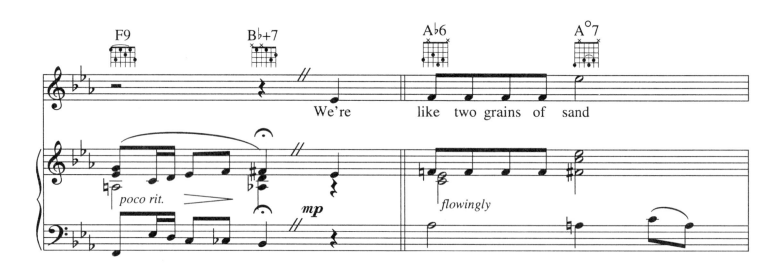

We're like two grains of sand

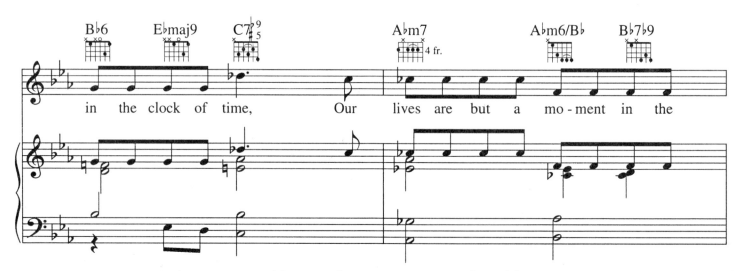

in the clock of time, Our lives are but a mo-ment in the

Each night, be-fore I wan-der off in-to sleep,

I'll bring to light the tears I've bur-ied so deep.

Then I'll kiss you, my dear,   Just as thoughyou were

1.   here.   2.   here.

rall.   *mp*

LET'S GET AWAY FROM IT ALL

Words by Tom Adair, Music by Matt Dennis

Let's take a kay - ak to Quin - cy or Ny - ack, Let's get a - way from it all.

Let's take a trip in a trail - er No need to come back at all

Let's take a pow - der to Bos - ton for chow - der,

Let's get a - way from it all. We'll tra - vel 'round from

LIKE SOMEONE IN LOVE

by Johnny Burke and Jimmy Van Heusen

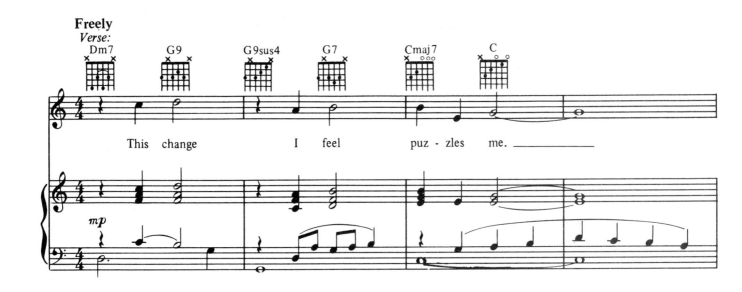

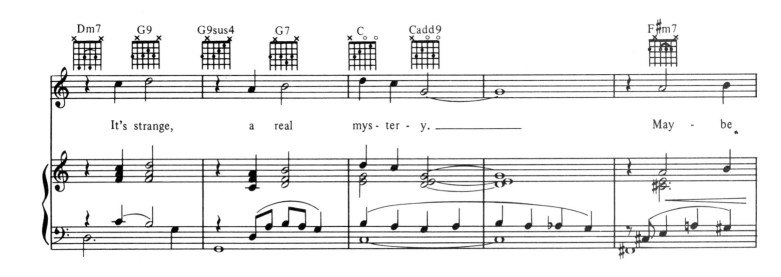

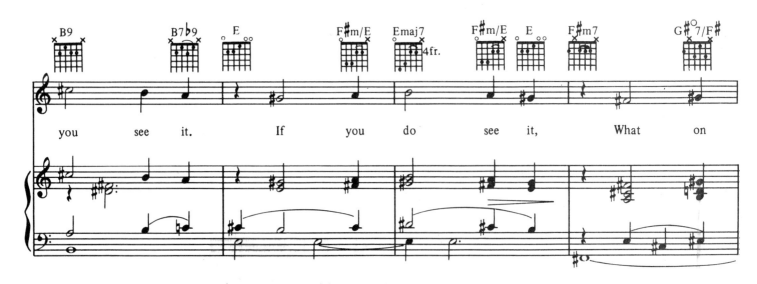

LUSH LIFE

by Billy Strayhorn

ME, MYSELF AND I

by Paul Vance and Al Byron

MY SUGAR IS SO REFINED

Music by Sid Lippman, Words by Sylvia Dee

* Substitute "he" for "she" and "him" for "her" for girl vocal throughout.

MY KINDA LOVE

Music by Louis Alter, Words by Jo Trent

don't be a dunce, When you meet it, steal it, beg or bor-row.

I'm fond o' you, You're fond o' me, Tell me you love me, and

hug me and squeeze me. My kind-a love, One way to par-a-

dise.

(THERE IS) NO GREATER LOVE

Music by Isham Jones, Words by Marty Symes

Freely, with expression

THE NIGHT WE CALLED IT A DAY

Words by Tom Adair, Music by Matt Dennis

185

NO MOON AT ALL

Music by Redd Evans, Words by David Mann

189

PERDIDO

Words by Ervin Drake and Harry Lenk, Music by Juan Tizol

OH, HOW I MISS YOU TONIGHT

by Benny Davis, Joseph Burke and Mark Fisher

Freely, with expression

197

OPUS ONE

Music by Sy Oliver, Words by Sid Garris and Sy Oliver

I'm wrack-in' my brain, to think of a name, To give to this tune, so Per-ry can croon And may-be Ol' Bing will give it a fling, And that-'ll start ev-'ry-one hum-min' the thing. The mel-o-dy's dumb, re-peat an' re-peat, But if you can swing, it's got a good beat, And

PERSONALITY

by Johnny Burke and Jimmy Van Heusen

all the books a-bout Du Bar-ry's looks What was it made her the toast_ of Par-ee?__
get some-where in spite of string-y hair_ Or e-ven just a bit bowed_ at the knee__

She had a well de - vel - oped
If she can show a fault - less

PER-SON-AL-I - TY. _____ And what did Ro - me - o see in
PER-SON-AL-I - TY. _____ And why are cer-tain girls of - fered

Jul - i - et, Or Pi - er - rot in Pi - er - rette, Or Jup - i - ter in
cer-tain things Like sab - le coats and wed-ding rings By men who wear their

202

PER-SON-AL-I-TY._____ A girl can
PER-SON-AL-I-TY.

POLKA DOTS AND MOONBEAMS

by Johnny Burke and Jimmy Van Heusen

Slowly, with expression
Chorus:

say it could-n't be true. A coun-try dance was be-ing

held in a gar-den, I felt a bump and heard an "Oh, beg your par-don,"

Sud-den-ly I saw pol - ka dots and moon-beams all a-round a pug-nosed dream.

The mus - ic start - ed and was I the per-plexed one,

205

And per-haps a few things more.___ Now in a cot-tage built of

li - lacs and laugh-ter, I know the mean-ing of the words, "ev - er af - ter."

And I'll al - ways see pol - ka dots and moon - beams

when I kiss the pug-nosed dream.___

SATIN DOLL

Music by Duke Ellington, Words by Billy Strayhorn and Johnny Mercer

that Sat - in Doll.___ She's no - bo - dy's fool, so I'm play - ing it cool as can be,___ I'll give it a whirl,— but I ain't for no girl___ catch - ing me.___ (Spoken:) Swich - e - Roo - ney

PRISONER OF LOVE

by Leo Robin, Russ Columbo and Clarence Gaskill

Knows that I have to be. Won-der if I am

wrong to Give {him/her} my loy-al-ty.

Why should I be a lone soul? Why can't I own my own soul?

Refrain

A-lone from night to night, you'll find me, Too weak to break the chains that

213

creep - ing; My ver - y life is in {his}{her} keep - ing,

I'm just a pris - 'ner of love. love.

SHOE SHINE BOY

Words by Sammy Cahn, Music by Saul Chaplin

like to sing your praise, but I don't know your name.

You're just a

Shoe shine boy, you work hard all day.

Shoe shine boy, got no time to play.

218

219

SLEIGH RIDE IN JULY

by Johnny Burke and Jimmy Van Heusen

way a - round, And what a time I had!

I was

tak - en for a sleigh ride in Ju - ly. ____

Oh, I must have been a set up for a

sigh. _____ A mock - ing - bird was

whist - ling a sen - ti - men - tal tune, And I

did - n't know e - nough to come in _____ out of the

moon - light. _____ So, the bigh ro - mance was

224

SHOW ME THE WAY TO
GET OUT OF THIS WORLD

Words by Les Clark, Music by Matt Dennis

Bb   Bb+   Bb6   Bbm7   Bbm6   C7b9   F

I'd go back and get 'em, but I have-n't the time. _
an - y-thing that's an - y good, they tell me is gone. _ } So, show me the way to get
ev - 'ry-thing is real - ly gone, I might as well go. __

F7   D7+   G9   Bb/C   1. F   C7+ 2. F

out of this world, _ 'Cause that's where ev - 'ry-thing is. ___   — At

Bb   B°7   F/C   D9   D/F#   G9

least, that's what they tell me when I ask where it is, ___ So, show me _____ the

C7   F   F13

way to get out of this world, _ 'Cause that's where ev - 'ry-thing is. ____

229

SOMEWHERE ALONG THE WAY

by Sammy Gallop and Kurt Adams

231

SUDDENLY
(Instrumentally known as IN WALKED BUD)

Music by Thelonious Monk, Lyrics by Jon Hendricks

Diz - zy, he was scream-in' next to O. P. who was beam-in', Monk was thump-in', Sud-den-ly in walked Bud, and then they got in - to some - thin'. Os - car played a mean sax, Mis - ter By - as blew a mean ax, Monk was

thump - in', Sud-den - ly in walked Bud, and then the joint start - ed

jump - in'. Ev - 'ry hip stud real - ly dug Bud soon's he hit

town, _____ Tak - in' that note no - bod -

y wrote, put - tin' it down. _____

O. P. he was scream-in' next to Diz - zy who was

beam - in', Monk was thump-in', Sud-den - ly in walked Bud, and

then they got in - to some - thin'.

SNOOTIE LITTLE CUTIE

by Bobby Troup

SUNDAY, MONDAY OR ALWAYS

by Johnny Burke and Jimmy Van Heusen

SWINGING ON A STAR

by Johnny Burke and Jimmy Van Heusen

Moderately, with a bounce

Would you like to swing on a star, Car-ry moon-beams home in a jar, _____ And be bet-ter off than you

are,   Or would you rath-er be a mule?   A

mule is an an-i-mal with long fun-ny ears,   He kicks up at an-y-thing he
pig is an an-i-mal with dirt on his face,   His shoes are a ter-ri-ble dis-

hears.   His back is brawn-y and his brain is weak, __   He's
grace.   He's got no man-ners when he eats his food, __   He's

just plain stu-pid with a stub-born streak. And by the way, if you hate to go to
fat and la-zy and ex-treme-ly rude. But if you don't care a feath-er or a

fish won't do an - y- thing but swim in a brook, He can't write his name or read a

book. _____ To fool the peo -ple is his on - ly thought, _ And

though he's slip-per - y, he still gets caught. But then if that sort of life is what you

wish, You may grow up to be a fish. _____ And all the

TAKE THE 'A' TRAIN

by Billy Strayhorn

To _____ go to Sug-ar Hill 'way up in Har-lem. _____

If _____ you miss the "A" train, _____

You'll _____ find you've missed the quick-est way to

Har-lem. _____ Hur-ry, _____ get on now it's

THAT OLE DEVIL CALLED LOVE

by Allan Roberts and Doris Fisher

THAT'S MY DESIRE

Words by Carroll Loveday, Music by Helmy Kresa

THERE ARE SUCH THINGS

by Stanley Adams, Abel Baer and George W. Meyer

THERE! I'VE SAID IT AGAIN

Music by David Mann, Words by Redd Evans

more can I say?__ Be - lieve me,__ there's no oth-er way.__ I love you__ no

use to pre - tend.__ There! I've said it a - gain.__ I've said it.__ There's

no-thing to hide.__ It's bet-ter___ than burn-ing in - side.__ I love you.__ I

will to the end.__ There! I've said it a - gain.__ I've tried to drum up a

TIME OUT FOR TEARS

by Abe Schiff and Irving Berman

here's what I'll do: _____ I'm gon - na

spend my time __ and dance and dine, __ Play - ing with some - bod - y

now, _____ But there'll be time out for tears __ when ev - er I think __ of

you. _____

THIS LOVE OF MINE

by Frank Sinatra, Sol Parker and Henry Sanicola

Let it break. _____ I ask the sun ____ and the moon, _____ the stars that shine. _____ ____ What's to be-come of it, _____ this love of mine. _____ This love of

TUXEDO JUNCTION

Words by Buddy Feyne, Music by Erskine Hawkins, William Johnson and Julian Dash

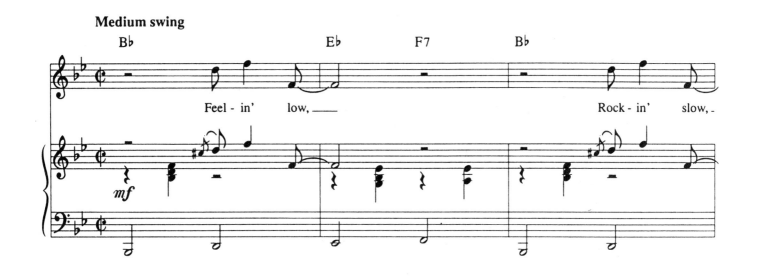

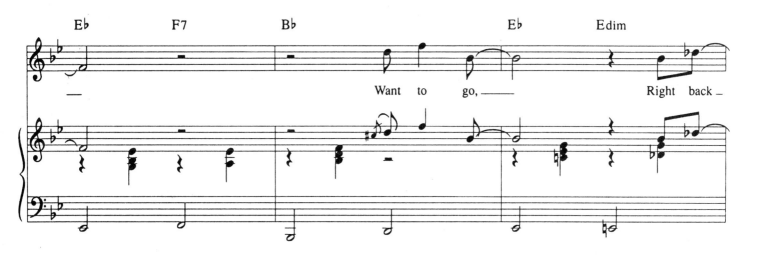

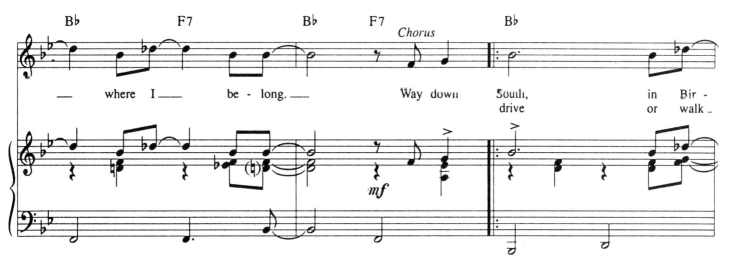

- ming - ham, ___ I mean South in Al - - a - bam's ___ an old
for miles, ___ to get jive that South - ern style, ___ S - low

place where peo - ple go ___ to dance ___ the night ___ a - way.
jive that makes ___ you want ___ to dance ___ 'til break ___ of day.

1.
___ They all ___

2.
It's a junc - tion where the town folks meet.

At each

UNDER A BLANKET OF BLUE

by Al Neiburg, Jerry Livingston and Marty Symes

sweet - heart, what a night for you and me.___

En - fold me, press your lips to mine and

hold me, It would be di - vine. Oh sweet - heart,

make this night a mem - o - ry._____

VIOLETS FOR YOUR FURS

by Tom Adair and Matt Dennis

Furs _____ and there was blue in the win - try sky,

You pinned the vi -o-lets to your furs _____ and gave a lift to the crowds pass - ing

by. You smiled at me so sweet - ly, Since

then one thought oc - curs, That we fell in love com-

plete-ly, The day that I bought you Vi -o -lets For Your Furs.   Furs.

WE'LL BE TOGETHER AGAIN

by Frankie Laine and Carl Fischer

287

WE'LL MEET AGAIN

by Ross Parker and Hughie Charles

set you, ___ I'll not for - get you, ___ sweet - heart.
mor - row, ___ Good-bye to sor - row, ___ my dear.

Moderately slow, with expression

Chorus

We'll meet a - gain, Don't know where, don't know

when, But I know we'll meet a - gain some sun - ny

WEAK FOR THE MAN

by Jeanne Burns

295

YES INDEED

by Sy Oliver

YOU CAN'T SEE THE SUN WHEN YOU'RE CRYING

by Allan Roberts and Doris Fisher

Moderately, with a beat

299

WILL YOU STILL BE MINE?

by Tom Adair and Matt Dennis

Chorus

When lov-ers make no ren-dez - vous _____ To stroll a - long Fifth Av-en-

ue _____ When this fa - mil-iar world is thru _____

Will you still be mine? _____ When cabs don't drive a-round the

park _____ No win-dows light the sum-mer dark _____

When love has lost its sec-ret spark _____ Will you still be mine?__

When moon-light on the Hud-son's not ro-man-cy ____
And spring no lon-ger turns a young man's fan-cy. When glam-our
girls have lost their charms ____ When si-rens just mean false a-
-larms ____ When lov-ers heed no call to arms ____ Will you
still be mine? ____ mine? ____

YOU ALWAYS HURT THE ONE YOU LOVE

by Allan Roberts and Doris Fisher

YOU DON'T HAVE TO
KNOW THE LANGUAGE

Words by Johnny Burke, Music by Jimmy Van Heusen

Moderately, with a swinging beat

But, you don't have to know the lan - guage With a

moon in the sky and a girl in your arms and a look in her eye.

When she smiles your____ way, What

more would you want an - y- one to say? So, you sigh, just____

YOU SAY YOU CARE
from GENTLEMEN PREFER BLONDES

Music by Jule Styne, Words by Leo Robin

quake. I'd prob-a-bly get you in dutch ___

with the Penn-syl-va-nia Dutch. ___ So I don't think I should

mar-ry you, I care for you too much.

YOU'VE GOT ME CRYING AGAIN

by Isham Jones and Charles Newman

Then it's all o - ver and in a lit - tle while:

poco a poco rit.

Moderately slow

You've got me cry - ing a - gain, You've got me sigh - ing a -

mf

gain. What is this love all a - bout, I'm

in, I'm out. Your kiss - es right from the

319